GREEK

HEART-WARMING TRADITIONAL RECIPES

Bounty
Books

CONTENTS

MEZZE

The many dishes of a mezze spread are designed to be shared. Two or three make a lovely pre-dinner snack with a drink; a selection of dishes is more often eaten as an entire meal.

EGGPLANT DIP

2 medium eggplants (600g)
¼ cup (60ml) olive oil
2 tablespoons finely chopped fresh flat-leaf parsley
½ small red onion (50g), chopped finely
1 medium ripe tomato (150g), chopped finely
1 tablespoon lemon juice

1 Stab eggplants all over with a fork. Grill eggplants over low flame of gas or barbecue until charred and tender. When eggplants are cool enough to handle, pull away and discard skin.

2 Coarsely chop eggplant flesh; combine with oil in large bowl. Stir in remaining ingredients; season to taste.

prep + cook time 25 minutes (+ cooling)
makes 2½ cups
nutritional count per tablespoon
1.9g total fat (0.3g saturated fat); 84kJ (20 cal); 0.6g carbohydrate; 0.3g protein; 0.5g fibre

serving suggestion Serve with pitta bread.

GRILLING THE EGGPLANT OVER A FLAME GIVES IT A SMOKY FLAVOUR. IF YOU FIND IT TOO MESSY, YOU CAN ALSO ROAST THEM IN THE OVEN OR IN A COVERED BARBECUE.

TARAMA IS SALT-CURED CARP OR COD ROE, AVAILABLE IN FISH SHOPS. THIS RECIPE USES MASHED POTATO BUT THERE ARE VARIATIONS USING BREAD SOAKED IN WATER. THE COLOUR OF THIS DIP CAN VARY FROM BEIGE TO PINK DEPENDING ON THE ROE [COMMERCIAL TARAMASALATA IS OFTEN COLOURED PINK].

TARAMASALATA

1 large potato (300g), chopped coarsely
90g (3 ounces) tarama
½ small white onion (40g), grated finely
¾ cup (180ml) extra light olive oil
¼ cup (60ml) white wine vinegar
1 tablespoon lemon juice

1 Boil, steam or microwave potato until tender; cool. Refrigerate until cold.
2 Mash potato in small bowl with tarama, onion, oil, vinegar and juice until smooth.

prep + cook time 25 minutes (+ refrigeration)
makes 1⅔ cups
nutritional count per tablespoon
10.7g total fat (1.6g saturated fat); 472kJ (113 cal); 2.6g carbohydrate; 1.6g protein; 0.3g fibre

serving suggestion Serve with toasted bread.

FETA AND SPINACH STUFFED POTATO BALLS

450g (14½ ounces) sebago potatoes,
  chopped coarsely
180g (5½ ounces) spinach, trimmed,
  shredded finely
150g (4½ ounces) feta cheese, crumbled
50g (1½ ounces) butter
⅔ cup (160ml) water
1 teaspoon salt
1 cup (150g) plain (all-purpose) flour
2 eggs
vegetable oil, for deep-frying

1 Boil, steam or microwave potato until tender;
drain. Mash potato in large bowl; cover to
keep warm.
2 Meanwhile, boil, steam or microwave spinach
until just wilted; drain. When cool enough to
handle, squeeze excess liquid from spinach.
Combine in medium bowl with cheese.
3 Melt butter in medium saucepan, add the
water and salt; bring to the boil. Remove from
heat; immediately stir in flour. Using a wooden
spoon, beat until mixture forms a smooth ball.
Beat in eggs and potato until smooth.
4 Using floured hands, roll level tablespoons
of dough into balls; use finger to press hole into
centre of each ball. Fill holes with level teaspoons
of spinach mixture; roll potato balls gently to
enclose filling.
5 Heat oil in large saucepan; deep-fry balls,
in batches, until browned lightly. Drain on
absorbent paper.

prep + cook time 1 hour 10 minutes
makes 30
nutritional count per ball
5.1g total fat (2g saturated fat); 293kJ (70 cal);
3.8g carbohydrate; 2.1g protein; 0.5g fibre

note You can also use lasoda or pink eye
potatoes for this recipe.

SPINACH AND CHEESE PARCELS

500g (1 pound) bunch spinach, trimmed, chopped finely

1 cup (80g) coarsely grated kefalotyri cheese

1 cup (200g) cottage cheese

2 tablespoons finely chopped fresh mint

1 egg

12 sheets filo pastry

2 tablespoons olive oil

1 Preheat oven to 220°C/425°F. Oil oven trays, line with baking paper.

2 Cook spinach in large frying pan until wilted; drain. When cool enough to handle, squeeze excess moisture from spinach. Combine spinach in medium bowl with cheeses, mint and egg; season.

3 Brush 1 sheet of pastry with oil; top with 3 more sheets, brushing each with oil. Cut layered sheets into quarters then cut quarters in half to make eight rectangles. Place 1 tablespoon of cheese mixture in centre of each rectangle. Fold in sides, leaving centre open. Repeat to make a total of 24 parcels.

4 Place parcels on tray; brush with oil.

5 Bake about 15 minutes or until browned lightly.

prep + cook time 45 minutes **makes** 24
nutritional count per parcel 3.3g total fat (1.2g saturated fat); 260kJ (62 cal); 4.6g carbohydrate; 3.5g protein; 0.4g fibre

WHEN WORKING WITH THE FIRST FOUR SHEETS OF PASTRY, COVER REMAINING PASTRY WITH A SHEET OF BAKING PAPER THEN A DAMP TEA TOWEL TO PREVENT IT DRYING OUT. YOU CAN ALSO MAKE THIS RECIPE WITH SILVER BEET; REMOVE THE WHITE STALKS AND VEINS FIRST.

TZATZIKI

500g (1 pound) Greek-style yogurt
1 lebanese cucumber (130g), peeled, grated coarsely
½ teaspoon salt
1 clove garlic, crushed
1 tablespoon lemon juice
2 tablespoons finely chopped fresh mint

1 Place yogurt onto large square of double-thickness muslin. Tie ends of muslin together; hang over large bowl, or place in a sieve to drain. Refrigerate about 2 hours or until yogurt is thick; discard liquid in bowl.
2 Meanwhile, combine cucumber and salt in small bowl; stand 20 minutes. Gently squeeze excess liquid from cucumber.
3 Combine yogurt and cucumber in small bowl with garlic, juice and mint; season to taste.

prep time 10 minutes (+ refrigeration)
makes 1¾ cups
nutritional count per tablespoon
1.7g total fat (1.1g saturated fat); 125kJ (30 cal); 2.3g carbohydrate; 1.4g protein; 0.1g fibre

MUSLIN, A COTTON CLOTH, IS AVAILABLE IN CRAFT AND COOKWARE SHOPS. THERE ARE MANY VARIATIONS OF THIS CLASSIC MEZZE: CUCUMBER CAN BE DICED INSTEAD OF GRATED. YOU CAN USE DILL AND PARSLEY INSTEAD OF MINT. IT'S A GREAT SIDE TO MOST MEAT DISHES.

YOU CAN VARY
THE HERBS OR
ADD FINELY
CHOPPED OLIVES,
IF YOU LIKE.

200g (6½ ounces) feta cheese
30g (1 ounce) unsalted butter, softened
2 tablespoons finely chopped fresh oregano
1 tablespoon finely chopped fresh mint
1 teaspoon finely grated lemon rind
2 teaspoons olive oil

1 Grease 1¼-cup (310ml) dish; line with plastic wrap.
2 Process cheese and butter until smooth. Transfer to medium bowl; stir in herbs and rind. Season with pepper. Press mixture firmly into dish. Cover; refrigerate 2 hours.
3 Unmould cheese onto plate; drizzle with oil.

prep time 15 minutes (+ refrigeration)
makes 1¼ cups
nutritional count per teaspoon 1.3g total fat (0.8g saturated fat); 60kJ (14 cal); 0g carbohydrate; 0.6g protein; 0g fibre

serving suggestions Serve with celery sticks and crusty bread.

HERBED FETA CHEESE

DOLMADES

2 tablespoons olive oil

2 medium brown onions (300g), chopped finely

155g (5 ounces) lean minced (ground) lamb

¾ cup (150g) white long-grain rice

2 tablespoons pine nuts

½ cup finely chopped fresh flat-leaf parsley

2 tablespoons each finely chopped fresh dill and mint

¼ cup (60ml) lemon juice

2 cups (500ml) water

500g (1 pound) preserved vine leaves

¾ cup (200g) yogurt

1 Heat oil in large saucepan; cook onion, stirring, until softened. Add lamb; cook, stirring, until browned. Stir in rice and pine nuts. Add herbs, 2 tablespoons of the juice and half the water; bring to the boil. Reduce heat; simmer, covered, 10 minutes or until water is absorbed and rice is partially cooked. Cool.

2 Rinse vine leaves in cold water. Drop leaves into a large saucepan of boiling water, in batches, for a few seconds, transfer to colander; rinse under cold water, drain well.

3 Place a vine leaf, smooth-side down on bench, trim large stem. Place a heaped teaspoon of rice mixture in centre. Fold stem end and sides over filling; roll up firmly. Line medium heavy-based saucepan with a few vine leaves; place rolls, close together, seam-side down, on leaves.

4 Pour over the remaining water; cover rolls with any remaining leaves. Place a plate on top of leaves to weigh down rolls. Cover pan tightly, bring to the boil. Reduce heat; simmer, over very low heat, 1½ hours. Remove from heat; stand, covered, about 2 hours or until liquid has been absorbed.

5 Serve dolmades with combined yogurt and remaining juice.

prep + cook time 3 hours (+ standing) **serves** 10
nutritional count per serving 7.6g total fat (1.6g saturated fat); 690kJ (165 cal); 14.9g carbohydrate; 7.7g protein; 3.2g fibre

FRIED CHILLI PRAWNS WITH GARLIC AND LEMON YOGURT

500g (1 pound) uncooked small prawns (shrimp)
1 cup (150g) plain (all-purpose) flour
1 teaspoon ground chilli
vegetable oil, for deep-frying

GARLIC AND LEMON YOGURT

¾ cup (210g) Greek-style yogurt
1 clove garlic, crushed
1 teaspoon finely grated lemon rind
1 tablespoon lemon juice

1 Make garlic and lemon yogurt.
2 Heat oil in medium saucepan or wok. Toss unshelled prawns in combined flour and chilli; shake away excess.
3 Deep-fry prawns, in batches, until browned lightly. Drain on absorbent paper. Season with salt and a little extra ground chilli.
4 Serve prawns with garlic and lemon yogurt.

garlic and lemon yogurt Combine ingredients in small bowl; season to taste.

prep + cook time 20 minutes
serves 6 as a starter
nutritional count per serving 8.2g total fat (2.7g saturated fat); 866kJ (207 cal); 12.9g carbohydrate; 20g protein; 0.7g fibre

serving suggestion Serve with lemon wedges.

SKORDALIA

3 medium potatoes (600g), unpeeled
3 cloves garlic
½ teaspoon salt
½ cup (125ml) olive oil
¼ cup (60ml) lemon juice
½ cup (125ml) milk

1 Boil, steam or microwave potatoes until tender. Drain.
2 Meanwhile, pound garlic and salt in a mortar and pestle until smooth, or, chop the garlic and salt together on a board and use the flat side of the knife blade to press garlic into a paste.
3 When potatoes are cool enough to handle, halve and spoon out flesh. Push flesh through sieve into large bowl. Whisk in oil, juice and garlic mixture then milk. Season with salt and white pepper.

prep + cook time 40 minutes **makes** 3 cups
nutritional count per tablespoon
3.3g total fat (0.6g saturated fat); 165kJ (39 cal); 2g carbohydrate; 0.5g protein; 0.3g fibre

serving suggestions Serve with pitta bread and raw vegetable sticks.

WE USED RUSSET DESIREE POTATOES. YOU CAN USE OTHER FLOURY VARIETIES SUCH AS KING EDWARD OR MARIS PIPER

PRAWN AND HALOUMI KEBABS

90g (3 ounces) haloumi cheese
18 small uncooked prawns (shrimp) (450g),
  shelled, de-veined
2 teaspoons rigani
2 tablespoons olive oil
6 bay leaves, halved

1 Cut cheese into 12 bite-sized pieces. Combine cheese, prawns, rigani and oil in shallow bowl. Thread prawns, bay leaves and cheese alternately onto six small skewers; season with pepper.
2 Cook skewers on heated grill plate (or grill or barbecue or grill pan) over medium-high heat until prawns are cooked through.

prep + cook time 20 minutes **makes** 6
nutritional count per skewer 8.9g total fat (2.7g saturated fat); 520kJ (124 cal); 0.3g carbohydrate; 10.9g protein; 0.1g fibre

serving suggestions Serve with lemon wedges and crusty bread.

GRILLED FETA AND BABY VINE TOMATOES

200g (6½ ounces) feta cheese
275g (9 ounces) baby vine tomatoes
1 tablespoon olive oil
1 teaspoon rigani

1 Preheat griller (broiler).
2 Place cheese and tomatoes on oven tray. Drizzle with oil; sprinkle with rigani. Season with pepper.
3 Place cheese and tomatoes under grill about 8 minutes or until cheese is browned lightly.

prep + cook time 10 minutes **serves** 4
nutritional count per serving 16g total fat (8.2g saturated fat); 796kJ (190 cal); 1.8g carbohydrate; 9.4g protein; 0.9g fibre

serving suggestion Serve with thinly sliced toasted bread stick.

TO STERILISE JARS: WASH THE JAR AND LID IN WARM SOAPY WATER; RINSE WELL. PLACE JAR IN LARGE SAUCEPAN AND COVER WITH WATER. BRING TO THE BOIL AND BOIL FOR 10 MINUTES. CAREFULLY DRAIN WATER FROM JARS; TRANSFER JAR AND LID TO A BAKING TRAY LINED WITH A CLEAN TEA TOWEL. COVER WITH A SHEET OF FOIL AND PLACE IN A LOW OVEN UNTIL DRY. USE STRAIGHT FROM THE OVEN. STORE MARINATED MUSHROOMS IN REFRIGERATOR FOR UP TO THREE MONTHS. SOMETIMES GARLIC WILL DISCOLOUR DURING STORAGE. THE GARLIC IS STILL EDIBLE – AND HARMLESS – IF THIS HAPPENS.

MARINATED MUSHROOMS

2 cups (500ml) white wine vinegar
½ cup (125ml) dry white wine
1 cup (250ml) water
4 bay leaves
2 tablespoons coarse cooking salt (kosher salt)
750g (1½ pounds) baby button mushrooms
4 cloves garlic, sliced thickly
1 teaspoon black peppercorns
3 sprigs rigani (Greek oregano)
1¼ cups (310ml) extra virgin olive oil

1 Sterilise 1 litre (4-cup) jar and lid.
2 Meanwhile, combine vinegar, wine, the water, bay leaves and salt in large saucepan; heat to simmer without boiling. Add mushrooms; simmer, uncovered, 10 minutes. Drain mushrooms, reserve bay leaves; discard liquid. Spread mushrooms in single layer on absorbent paper; stand 5 minutes.
3 Spoon mushrooms into hot sterilised jar with reserved bay leaves, garlic, peppercorns and rigani. Pour hot oil over mushrooms in jar, pressing on mushrooms with back of spoon to release any trapped air, leaving 1cm (½-inch) space between mushrooms and top of jar. Seal jar while hot.

prep + cook time 25 minutes (+ standing)
makes 4 cups
nutritional count per ¼ cup 1.9g total fat (0.3g saturated fat); 110kJ (26 cal); 0.7g carbohydrate; 1.6g protein; 0.7g fibre

EGGPLANT FRITTERS WITH GARLIC YOGURT

1 large eggplant (aubergine) (500g), cut into
thick lengths
1 tablespoon coarse cooking salt (kosher salt)
vegetable oil, for deep-frying
1 teaspoon rigani (Greek oregano)

OREGANO AND LEMON BATTER

½ cup (75g) plain (all-purpose) flour
⅔ cup (160ml) beer
1 tablespoon rigani
1 teaspoon finely grated lemon rind

GARLIC YOGURT

1 cup (280g) Greek-style yogurt
1 clove garlic, crushed
1 tablespoon finely chopped fresh dill

1 Place eggplant in colander over bowl, sprinkle
with salt; stand 1 hour.
2 Meanwhile, make oregano and lemon batter.
3 Make garlic yogurt.
4 Heat oil in large saucepan or wok. Rinse
eggplant under cold water, pat dry with
absorbent paper. Dip eggplant into batter, shake
away excess. Deep-fry eggplant, in batches,
turning occasionally, about 5 minutes or until
browned. Drain on absorbent paper.
5 Sprinkle eggplant with rigani and a little salt;
serve with garlic yogurt.

oregano and lemon batter Sift flour into large
bowl, gradually whisk in beer until batter is
smooth. Add rigani and rind; season. Stand 1
hour.

garlic yogurt Combine ingredients in small
bowl; season to taste.

prep + cook time 40 minutes (+ standing)
serves 4
nutritional count per serving 18g total fat (4.4g
saturated fat); 1295kJ (309 cal); 27g
carbohydrate; 6.9g protein; 4g fibre

DEEP-FRIED BABY CALAMARI

500g (1 pound) baby calamari, cleaned
⅓ cup (50g) plain (all-purpose) flour
vegetable oil, for deep-frying
2 teaspoons rigani

1 Slice calamari into thin rings. Season flour with salt and pepper.
2 Heat oil in medium saucepan or wok. Toss calamari in flour mixture; shake away excess. Deep-fry calamari, in batches, until browned lightly and tender. Drain on absorbent paper.
3 Sprinkle calamari with rigani; serve with a squeeze of lemon juice.

prep + cook time 15 minutes **serves** 4
nutritional count per serving 4g total fat (0.6g saturated fat); 425kJ (100 cal); 6.4g carbohydrate; 9.9g protein; 0.4g fibre

serving suggestion Serve with lemon wedges.

DON'T OVERCOOK THE CALAMARI OR IT WILL TOUGHEN. IT SHOULD TAKE ABOUT 30 SECONDS TO COOK ONE SMALL BATCH AT A TIME. REHEAT THE OIL BEFORE FRYING THE NEXT BATCH OF CALAMARI. ASK THE FISHMONGER TO CLEAN THE CALAMARI FOR YOU.

THYME AND GARLIC MARINATED OLIVES

1 medium lemon (140g)
½ cup (125ml) olive oil
2 cloves garlic, bruised
3 sprigs fresh thyme
1 bay leaf
2 cups (320g) large kalamata olives, rinsed, drained

1 Sterilise jar and lid.
2 Meanwhile, using a vegetable peeler, peel rind thinly from lemon, avoiding white pith. Combine rind, oil, garlic, thyme and bay leaf in medium saucepan over medium heat; heat until warm and garlic begins to sizzle. Add olives; cook over low heat 10 minutes.
3 Spoon hot olives into sterilised jar. Seal jar while hot.

prep + cook time 15 minutes **serves** 12
nutritional count per serving 7.4g total fat (1g saturated fat); 295kJ (70 cal); 0.6g carbohydrate; 0.4g protein; 0.7g fibre

TO STERILISE JARS: WASH THE JAR AND LID IN WARM SOAPY WATER; RINSE WELL. PLACE JAR IN LARGE SAUCEPAN AND COVER WITH WATER. BRING TO THE BOIL AND BOIL FOR 10 MINUTES. CAREFULLY DRAIN WATER FROM JARS; TRANSFER JAR AND LID TO A BAKING TRAY LINED WITH A CLEAN TEA TOWEL. COVER WITH A SHEET OF FOIL AND PLACE IN A LOW OVEN UNTIL DRY. USE STRAIGHT FROM THE OVEN.

SPANAKOPITA

1.5kg (3 pounds) silver beet (swiss chard), trimmed
1 tablespoon olive oil
1 medium brown onion (150g), chopped finely
2 cloves garlic, crushed
1 teaspoon ground nutmeg
200g (6½ ounces) feta cheese, crumbled
1 tablespoon finely grated lemon rind
¼ cup each coarsely chopped fresh mint, fresh dill
   and fresh flat-leaf parsley
4 spring onions (scallions), chopped finely
16 sheets filo pastry
125g (4 ounces) butter, melted
2 teaspoons sesame seeds

1 Boil, steam or microwave silver beet until just wilted; drain. Squeeze out excess moisture; drain on absorbent paper. Chop silver beet coarsely; spread out on absorbent paper.
2 Heat oil in small frying pan; cook brown onion and garlic, stirring, until onion is soft. Add nutmeg; cook, stirring, until fragrant. Combine onion mixture and silver beet in large bowl with feta, rind, herbs and green onion.
3 Preheat oven to 180°C/350°F. Oil oven trays.
4 Brush 1 sheet of pastry with some of the butter; fold lengthways into thirds, brushing with butter between each fold. Place a rounded tablespoon of silver beet mixture at the bottom of one narrow edge of folded pastry sheet, leaving a border. Fold one corner of pastry diagonally over filling to form a large triangle. Continue folding to end of pastry sheet, retaining triangular shape. Repeat with remaining ingredients to make 16 triangles in total.
5 Place triangles, seam-side down, on trays. Brush with remaining butter; sprinkle with sesame seeds. Bake about 15 minutes or until browned lightly.

prep + cook time 50 minutes **makes** 16
nutritional count per triangle 11.1g total fat (6.4g saturated fat); 690kJ (165 cal); 11g carbohydrate; 4.7g protein; 1.5g fibre

SPANAKOPITA COMES FROM THE GREEK WORDS SPANAKI [SPINACH] AND PITTA [PIE]. WHEN WORKING WITH THE FIRST SHEET OF PASTRY, COVER REMAINING PASTRY WITH A SHEET OF BAKING PAPER THEN A DAMP TEA TOWEL TO PREVENT IT FROM DRYING OUT.

GRILLED HALOUMI

500g (1 pound) haloumi cheese
2 tablespoons lemon juice
1 tablespoon coarsely chopped fresh flat-leaf parsley

1 Cut cheese into 1cm (½-inch) slices. Cook cheese on heated oiled flat plate until browned both sides.
2 Transfer cheese to serving plate; drizzle with juice. Serve immediately, sprinkled with parsley.

prep + cook time 10 minutes **serves** 6
nutritional count per serving 14.3g total fat (9.2g saturated fat); 861kJ (206 cal); 1.7g carbohydrate; 17.8g protein; 0g fibre

HALOUMI IS BEST COOKED
JUST BEFORE SERVING AS
IT BECOMES TOUGH AND
RUBBERY ON COOLING.

USE DISPOSABLE GLOVES WHEN
HANDLING BEETROOT TO PREVENT
YOUR HANDS BECOMING STAINED.

BEETROOT SALAD

500g (1 pound) bunch baby beetroot
2 tablespoons olive oil
1 tablespoon red wine vinegar
1 tablespoon finely chopped fresh flat-leaf parsley
1 teaspoon finely chopped fresh dill
1 clove garlic, crushed

1 Discard leaves from beetroot; reserve stems. Wash beetroot and stems. Place beetroots in medium saucepan; cover with water. Bring to the boil; simmer, covered, about 30 minutes or until tender. Add stems 5 minutes before end of cooking time. Drain.
2 When beetroots are cool enough to handle, use disposable gloves to gently slip off skin from beetroots; discard skins. Slice beetroots and stems.
3 Place beetroot and stems in shallow bowl with combined remaining ingredients; toss gently. Season to taste.

prep + cook time 40 minutes (+ cooling)
serves 4
nutritional count per serving 4.6g total fat (0.7g saturated fat); 260kJ (62 cal); 4.3g carbohydrate; 1g protein; 2g fibre

CHEESE FILO TRIANGLES

1 cup (200g) cottage cheese
100g (3 ounces) feta cheese
1 egg
2 tablespoons each finely chopped
  fresh oregano and fresh flat-leaf parsley
15 sheets filo pastry
¼ cup (60ml) olive oil

1 Preheat oven to 220°C/425°F. Oil oven trays, line with baking paper.
2 Combine cheeses, egg and herbs in medium bowl; season with pepper.
3 Brush 1 sheet of pasty with some of the oil; top with 2 more sheets, brushing each with more oil. Cut layered sheets into three strips lengthways. Place 1 level tablespoon of cheese mixture at one narrow edge of each pastry strip. Fold one corner of pastry diagonally over filling to form a triangle. Continue folding to end of strip, retaining triangular shape. Repeat to make 15 triangles.
4 Place triangles, seam-side down, on trays; brush with a little more oil.
5 Bake triangles about 15 minutes or until browned lightly.

prep + cook time 30 minutes **makes** 15
nutritional count per triangle 6.5g total fat
(2.2g saturated fat); 480kJ (115 cal); 9g
carbohydrate; 5g protein; 0.4g fibre

WHEN WORKING WITH THE FIRST THREE
SHEETS OF PASTRY, COVER REMAINING
PASTRY WITH A SHEET OF BAKING
PAPER THEN A DAMP TEA TOWEL TO
PREVENT IT FROM DRYING OUT.

ZUCCHINI FRITTERS WITH SKORDALIA

4 medium zucchini (courgettes) (480g)
2 teaspoons coarse cooking salt (kosher salt)
peanut oil, for deep-frying

SKORDALIA

4 slices stale white sandwich bread (180g),
    crusts removed
4 cloves garlic, crushed
½ cup (125ml) olive oil
1 tablespoon lemon juice
1 tablespoon water, approximately

BATTER

1 cup (150g) self-raising flour
¾ cup (180ml) warm water
1 tablespoon olive oil
1 egg yolk

1 Make skordalia.
2 Cut zucchini into 1cm (½-inch) diagonal slices.
Place zucchini in colander, sprinkle with salt;
stand 30 minutes. Rinse zucchini under cold
water; drain on absorbent paper.
3 Make batter.
4 Dip zucchini into batter, carefully lower into
hot oil; cook zucchini until browned and crisp.
Drain on absorbent paper.
5 Serve zucchini with skordalia.

skordalia Briefly dip bread into a bowl of cold
water, then gently squeeze out the water. Blend
or process bread and garlic until combined.
With motor operating, gradually add oil, juice
and enough of the water, in a thin steady stream,
until mixture is smooth and thick. Transfer to
serving bowl.

batter Sift flour into medium bowl; whisk in
combined remaining ingredients until smooth.
Stand batter 10 minutes. If batter thickens too
much, whisk in a little extra water to give it a
coating consistency.

prep + cook time 1 hour (+ standing) **serves** 6
nutritional count per serving 28g total fat
(4.2g saturated fat); 1601kJ (383 cal);
26.5g carbohydrate; 5.4g protein; 3g fibre

HARVEST OF THE SEA

With 20 per cent of Greece made up of islands and no part of the mainland more than a few hundred kilometres from the sea, fish and seafood are an important part of Greek cuisine.

PRAWN SOUVLAKIA WITH TOMATO AND FENNEL SAUCE

16 large uncooked prawns (shrimp) (1.1kg)
2 tablespoons olive oil
3 cloves garlic, crushed
2 teaspoons dried mint
1 teaspoon finely grated lemon rind
2 tablespoons lemon juice

TOMATO AND FENNEL SAUCE

2 baby fennel bulbs (260g)
1 tablespoon olive oil
1 medium brown onion (150g), chopped finely
2 cloves garlic, chopped finely
3 medium ripe tomatoes (450g), chopped coarsely
¼ cup (60ml) ouzo or pernod
1 cup coarsely chopped fresh mint

1 Shell and de-vein prawns, leaving tails intact. Place prawns in large bowl with remaining ingredients; toss to combine. Cover; refrigerate 1 hour.
2 Make tomato and fennel sauce.
3 Thread prawns onto eight metal skewers; reserve marinade. Cook prawn skewers on heated oiled grill plate (or grill or barbecue or grill pan), brushing with reserved marinade, until cooked through.
4 Serve prawns with sauce.

tomato and fennel sauce Reserve fennel fronds; chop fennel and fronds finely, separately. Heat oil in medium saucepan over medium heat; cook onion, garlic and fennel until softened. Add tomato and ouzo; cook until heated through. Just before serving, stir in fronds and mint; season.

prep + cook time 35 minutes (+ refrigeration)
makes 8
nutritional count per skewer 7.5g total fat (1.3g saturated fat); 702kJ (168 cal); 5.9g carbohydrate; 15.4g protein; 2g fibre

serving suggestion Serve with rice pilaf.

BARBECUED VINE-LEAF-WRAPPED SARDINES

12 small whole sardines (500g), cleaned
1 medium lemon (140g), halved, sliced thinly
12 fresh bay leaves
12 small preserved vine leaves
1 tablespoon olive oil

GARLIC AND LEMON POTATOES

2 tablespoons olive oil
600g (1¼ pounds) small potatoes, sliced thinly
1 medium lemon (140g)
4 cloves garlic, sliced thinly

PRESERVED VINE LEAVES ARE AVAILABLE IN CRYOVAC PACKETS FROM SOME DELICATESSENS AND MIDDLE EASTERN FOOD SHOPS; THEY MUST BE RINSED WELL AND DRIED BEFORE USING.

1 Rinse cavities of sardines, pat dry. Season cavities; top each sardine with a lemon slice and a bay leaf. Wrap each sardine tightly in a vine leaf to enclose lemon and bay leaf, leaving head and tail exposed. Brush sardines with oil.
2 Make garlic and lemon potatoes.
3 Meanwhile, cook sardines on heated oiled grill plate (or grill or barbecue or grill pan), until cooked through.
4 Serve sardines with potatoes and lemon wedges.

garlic and lemon potatoes Heat oil in large frying pan; cook potatoes, turning, about 15 minutes until starting to soften and brown. Remove rind from whole lemon using a zester, add to potatoes with garlic; cook, stirring, until potatoes and garlic are cooked through. Season to taste.

prep + cook time 1 hour **serves** 4
nutritional count per serving 20g total fat (3.9g saturated fat); 1686kJ (403 cal); 17g carbohydrate; 37.9g protein; 3.6g fibre

serving suggestion Serve with sliced tomato and white onion salad.

BAKED FISH WITH TOMATO AND OLIVES

4 x 260g (8½-ounce) whole white fish
1 tablespoon olive oil
2 medium red onions (340g), sliced thinly
2 stalks celery (300g), trimmed, sliced thinly
4 cloves garlic, sliced thinly
400g (12½ ounces) cherry tomatoes
¾ cup (120g) seeded black olives
1 medium lemon (140g), halved, sliced thinly
¼ cup fresh rosemary sprigs
1 cup (250ml) dry white wine
½ cup coarsely chopped fresh flat-leaf parsley

1 Preheat oven to 200°C/400°F.
2 Remove heads from fish; clean fish.
3 Heat oil in medium baking dish; cook onion, celery and garlic, stirring, until browned lightly. Add tomatoes, olives, lemon and rosemary.
4 Season fish; place on vegetables. Pour wine over fish. Roast, uncovered, about 15 minutes or until fish is cooked through.
5 Serve fish sprinkled with parsley.

prep + cook time 40 minutes **serves** 4
nutritional count per serving 2.9g total fat (0.5g saturated fat); 253kJ (60 cal); 1.8g carbohydrate; 5.9g protein; 1.3g fibre

serving suggestions Serve with potatoes, pasta or rice salad.

PRAWNS WITH ZUCCHINI AND MINT PILAF

20 uncooked medium prawns (shrimp) (1kg)
60g (2 ounces) butter
1 tablespoon olive oil
1 medium white onion (150g), chopped finely
2 cloves garlic, chopped finely
1 fresh small red chilli, chopped finely
1½ cups (300g) white long-grain rice
1 teaspoon finely grated lemon rind
¼ cup (60ml) dry white wine
1½ cups (375ml) hot fish stock
3 medium zucchini (courgette) (360g),
   grated coarsely

MINTED LEMON DRESSING

2 medium lemons (280g), peeled, segmented
1 cup loosely packed fresh flat-leaf parsley leaves
½ cup loosely packed fresh mint leaves
¼ cup (60ml) olive oil

1 Shell and de-vein prawns, leaving tails intact; refrigerate.
2 Heat butter and oil in medium heavy-based saucepan; cook onion, garlic and chilli, stirring, until onion softens. Add rice, rind and wine; cook until liquid has evaporated. Stir in hot stock, bring to the boil. Reduce heat to low, stirring; cook, covered, 10 minutes.
3 Meanwhile, make minted lemon dressing.
4 Stir zucchini into rice mixture; top with prawns. Cover; cook 5 minutes. Remove from heat; stand, covered, 5 minutes.
5 Serve pilaf drizzled with dressing.

minted lemon dressing Process ingredients until chopped finely. Season to taste.

prep + cook time 40 minutes (+ standing)
serves 4
nutritional count per serving 32.3g total fat (11.2g saturated fat); 2880kJ (688 cal); 64.2g carbohydrate; 33.2g protein; 4.6g fibre

SQUID STUFFED WITH RICE, CURRANTS AND PINE NUTS

12 small squid (800g)
¼ cup (60ml) olive oil
1 medium onion (150g), chopped finely
2 cloves garlic, chopped finely
½ cup (100g) white long-grain rice
¾ cup (180ml) fish stock
2 tablespoons dried currants
2 tablespoons roasted pine nuts
25g (¾ ounce) baby spinach leaves, sliced thinly
1 tablespoon finely shredded fresh mint leaves
1 teaspoon finely grated lemon rind
2 tablespoons lemon juice

1 Clean squid; reserve tentacles and wing. Cut tentacles and wings into small pieces.
2 Heat 1 tablespoon of the oil in medium heavy-based saucepan; cook onion and garlic, stirring, until onion softens. Add rice; stir to coat in onion mixture. Stir in squid pieces, stock, currants and pine nuts. Simmer, covered tightly, about 10 minutes or until liquid has evaporated and rice is tender.
3 Stir spinach leaves, mint, rind and juice into rice mixture; season. Spoon rounded tablespoons mixture into squid tubes leaving 1cm (½-inch) gap; secure ends with toothpicks.
4 Preheat oven to 180°C/350°F.
5 Heat remaining oil in large frying pan; cook squid, in batches, until browned lightly. Transfer squid to oven tray, roast uncovered, about 5 minutes or until squid is opaque and filling is heated through.

prep + cook time 1 hour **serves** 4
nutritional count per serving 20.2g total fat (2.9g saturated fat); 1505kJ (360 cal); 26.6g carbohydrate; 18.3g protein; 2.1g fibre

serving suggestion Serve with a baby rocket salad.

OCTOPUS IN RED WINE

1.5kg (3 pounds) octopus tentacles
1½ cups (375ml) dry red wine
¼ cup (60ml) red wine vinegar
¼ cup (60ml) olive oil
2 cloves garlic, sliced thinly
2 bay leaves
1 fresh small red chilli, sliced
1 cinnamon stick
2 teaspoons whole allspice
2 strips lemon rind
1½ cups (375ml) water
12 baby brown pickling onions (240g)
8 baby new potatoes (240g)
1 cup coarsely chopped fresh flat-leaf parsley

1 Preheat oven to 120°C/250°F.
2 Combine octopus, wine, vinegar, oil, garlic, bay leaves, chilli, cinnamon, allspice, rind and the water in large deep flameproof dish. Cook, covered, in oven, 1 hour. Add onions to dish; cook, covered, about 30 minutes or until tender.
3 Remove octopus and onions from dish. Bring liquid in dish to the boil; add potatoes, simmer, uncovered, about 20 minutes or until potatoes are tender. Remove potatoes, cut in half. Simmer sauce, uncovered, about 15 minutes or until sauce is reduced to about 2 cups.
4 Meanwhile, thickly slice octopus.
5 Add octopus to sauce with onions and potatoes; cook until heated through. Just before serving, add parsley. Season to taste.

prep + cook time 2 hours 20 minutes **serves** 6
nutritional count per serving 11.7g total fat (2g saturated fat); 1421kJ (339 cal); 12.5g carbohydrate; 65.6g protein; 2.3g fibre

serving suggestion Serve with crusty bread.

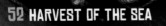

CRISP-SKINNED FISH WITH ROAST GARLIC SKORDALIA

4 x 200g (6½-ounce) white fish fillets, skin on

ROSEMARY OIL

¼ cup (60ml) olive oil
4 cloves garlic, sliced thinly
2 tablespoons rosemary

ROAST GARLIC SKORDALIA

2 medium bulbs garlic (140g)
600g (1¼ pounds) small potatoes
½ cup (125ml) milk, warmed
1 tablespoon finely grated lemon rind
½ cup (125ml) olive oil
½ cup (140g) Greek-style yogurt
¼ cup (60ml) lemon juice

WE USED BARRAMUNDI IN THIS RECIPE, BUT ANY WHITE FISH FILLETS WOULD BE FINE.

1 Make rosemary oil and roast garlic skordalia.
2 Pat fish dry with absorbent paper; season. Heat 1 tablespoon of the rosemary oil in medium frying pan; cook fish, skin-side down, about 2 minutes or until skin is crisp. Turn fish, cook fish through.
3 Serve fish with skordalia and drizzled with rosemary oil.

rosemary oil Heat oil, garlic and rosemary in small saucepan over low heat until garlic begins to colour. Remove from heat; cool.

roast garlic skordalia Preheat oven to 220°C/425°F. Wrap garlic in foil; place on oven tray with potatoes. Roast about 30 minutes or until garlic and potatoes are soft. Stand until cool enough to handle. Peel potatoes; place flesh in medium bowl. Squeeze garlic from cloves, add to potatoes with half the warm milk. Mash rind, garlic and potatoes until smooth. Gradually stir in oil, 1 tablespoon at a time. Stir in yogurt and juice; season to taste. Just before serving, heat remaining milk in medium saucepan; add skordalia, cook, stirring, until heated through.

prep + cook time 1 hour (+ cooling) **serves** 4
nutritional count per serving 53.4g total fat (11g saturated fat); 3210kJ (767 cal); 24g carbohydrate; 47.7g protein; 6.7g fibre

VILLAGE FAVOURITES

Greek hospitality is legendary and everyone's invited. The table is spread with an abundance of food, lovingly prepared and generously shared with family, friends and strangers alike.

SLOW-ROASTED LAMB WITH SKORDALIA AND POTATOES

2kg (4-pound) leg of lamb
2 cloves garlic, crushed
½ cup (125ml) lemon juice
2 tablespoons olive oil
1 tablespoon fresh oregano leaves
2 teaspoons fresh lemon thyme leaves
5 large potatoes (1.5kg), chopped coarsely
1 tablespoon finely grated lemon rind
2 tablespoons lemon juice, extra
2 tablespoons olive oil, extra

SKORDALIA

1 medium potato (200g), quartered
3 cloves garlic, crushed
1 tablespoon lemon juice
1 tablespoon white wine vinegar
2 tablespoons water
⅓ cup (80ml) olive oil

1 Combine lamb, garlic, juice, oil, oregano and half the thyme in large bowl. Cover; refrigerate 3 hours or overnight.
2 Preheat oven to 160°C/325°F.
3 Place lamb mixture in large baking dish; roast, uncovered, 3 hours.
4 Meanwhile, make skordalia.
5 Combine potatoes, rind, extra juice, extra oil and remaining thyme in large bowl. Place potatoes, in single layer, on oven tray. Roast potatoes, uncovered, for last 30 minutes of lamb cooking time.
6 Remove lamb from oven; cover to keep warm.
7 Increase oven to 220°C/425°F; roast potatoes a further 20 minutes or until browned lightly and cooked through.
8 Serve lamb and potatoes with skordalia and pan juices.

skordalia Boil, steam or microwave potato until tender; drain. Push potato through fine sieve into medium bowl; cool 10 minutes. Whisk combined garlic, juice, vinegar and the water into potato. Gradually whisk in oil in a thin, steady stream; continue whisking until skordalia thickens. Stir in about a tablespoon of warm water if skordalia becomes too thick.

prep + cook time 4 hours (+ refrigeration)
serves 4
nutritional count per serving 57g total fat (14g saturated fat); 4556kJ (1090 cal); 51.5g carbohydrate; 91.2g protein; 6.7g fibre

RABBIT STIFADO

ASK THE BUTCHER TO CHOP THE RABBIT INTO PIECES FOR YOU.

1.4kg (2¾-pound) whole rabbit

⅔ cup (160ml) dry red wine

⅓ cup (80ml) red wine vinegar

2 cloves garlic, crushed

3 bay leaves

1 cinnamon stick

6 cloves

1 tablespoon light brown sugar

2 teaspoons rigani

½ teaspoon ground allspice

¼ cup (60ml) olive oil

800g (1½ pounds) baby brown onions, peeled

2 tablespoons tomato paste

1 litre (4 cups) water

2 tablespoons coarsely chopped fresh
  flat-leaf parsley

1 Chop rabbit into eight even-sized pieces. Combine rabbit, wine, vinegar, garlic, bay leaves, cinnamon, cloves, sugar, rigani and allspice in large bowl. Cover; refrigerate 3 hours or overnight.

2 Heat oil in large saucepan; cook onions, stirring, over medium heat, until softened. Remove from pan.

3 Remove rabbit from marinade; reserve marinade. Cook rabbit in same heated pan, in batches, until browned. Remove from pan.

4 Return rabbit and onions to pan with paste, the water and reserved marinade; bring to the boil. Reduce heat; simmer, uncovered, over low heat, about 2 hours or until sauce has thickened. Season.

prep + cook time 2 hours 35 minutes
(+ refrigeration) **serves** 4
nutritional count per serving 27.9g total fat
(5.7g saturated fat); 2284kJ (546 cal);
12.8g carbohydrate; 54.3g protein; 4.6g fibre

serving suggestion Crusty bread.

GREEK SALAD

¼ cup (60ml) olive oil
1 tablespoon lemon juice
1 tablespoon white wine vinegar
1 tablespoon finely chopped fresh oregano
1 clove garlic, crushed
3 medium tomatoes (450g), cut into wedges
2 lebanese cucumbers (260g), chopped coarsely
200g (6½ ounces) feta cheese, chopped coarsely
1 small red capsicum (bell pepper) (150g),
  sliced thinly
1 small red onion (100g), sliced thinly
½ cup (75g) seeded black olives

1 Whisk oil, juice, vinegar, oregano and garlic in large bowl.
2 Add remaining ingredients to bowl; toss gently to combine.

prep time 20 minutes **serves** 4
nutritional count per serving 25.8g total fat (9.6g saturated fat); 1359kJ (325 cal); 10.8g carbohydrate; 11.5g protein; 3.2g fibre

EGGPLANT SALAD

1 large eggplant (aubergine) (500g)

PARSLEY DRESSING

¼ cup coarsely chopped fresh flat-leaf parsley
1 clove garlic, crushed
1 teaspoon rigani
2 tablespoons olive oil
1 tablespoon lemon juice

1 Preheat oven to 200°C/400°F.
2 Place eggplant on oven tray; prick all over with a fork. Roast eggplant about 40 minutes, turning occasionally, until very soft. Cool; peel.
3 Meanwhile, make parsley dressing.
4 Tear eggplant flesh into long strips; arrange on serving plate. Serve with dressing.

parsley dressing Combine ingredients in small bowl; season to taste.

prep + cook time 50 minutes (+ cooling)
serves 4 as a side
nutritional count per serving 9.5g total fat (1.5g saturated fat); 424kJ (101 cal); 3.1g carbohydrate; 1.3g protein; 3.1g fibre

ROASTED GARLIC LEMON AND OREGANO CHICKEN

1.5kg (3 pounds) medium potatoes,
  quartered lengthways
4 chicken marylands (1.4kg)
½ cup (125ml) lemon juice
½ cup (125ml) olive oil
6 cloves garlic, chopped finely
2 teaspoons rigani
1½ cups (375ml) water

1 Preheat oven to 180°C/350°F.
2 Place potatoes in large baking dish; top with
chicken. Combine juice, oil, garlic and rigani
in small jug; pour over chicken and potatoes.
Add the water to dish; season with salt and
ground white pepper.
3 Roast chicken and potatoes, uncovered, about
1½ hours or until chicken is tender and browned.

prep + cook time 1 hour 40 minutes **serves** 4
nutritional count per serving 46.2g total fat (9.8g
saturated fat); 3793kJ (906 cal); 48.1g carbohydrate;
73.5g protein; 7.3g fibre

serving suggestion Serve with a green salad.

LENTIL SOUP

1 tablespoon olive oil
1 medium brown onion (150g), chopped finely
2 cloves garlic, crushed
1 cup (200g) brown lentils, rinsed, drained
400g (12½ ounces) canned diced tomatoes
1½ cups (375ml) chicken stock
1½ cups (375ml) water
1 bay leaf
2 tablespoons coarsely chopped fresh dill

1 Heat oil in large saucepan; cook onion, stirring, until softened. Stir in garlic; cook until fragrant.
2 Stir in lentils, undrained tomatoes, stock, the water and bay leaf; bring to the boil. Reduce heat; simmer, covered, about 50 minutes or until lentils are tender. Season to taste. Discard bay leaf.
3 Serve soup topped with dill.

prep + cook time 1 hour **serves** 4
nutritional count per serving 6.2g total fat (1g saturated fat); 880kJ (210 cal); 25.3g carbohydrate; 14.2g protein; 9.2g fibre

serving suggestions Serve with a dash of red wine vinegar for each bowl and crusty bread.

BRAISED BORLOTTI BEANS WITH TOMATO AND GARLIC

500g (1 pound) fresh borlotti beans, shelled
⅓ cup (80ml) olive oil
1 cup (250ml) water
1 bulb garlic, cut in half horizontally
3 large ripe tomatoes (450g), chopped coarsely
¼ cup fresh oregano leaves
½ cup coarsely chopped fresh basil

1 Preheat oven to 180°C/350°F.
2 Place beans in medium baking dish; drizzle with oil and the water. Add garlic, tomato and oregano.
3 Bake beans, covered, about 1¼ hours or until beans are tender. Just before serving, stir in basil.

prep + cook time 1 hour 25 minutes **serves** 4
nutritional count per serving 18.4g total fat (2.6g saturated fat); 752kJ (180 cal); 2.3g carbohydrate; 1.2g protein; 1.6g fibre

BROAD BEANS AND ARTICHOKES

300g (9½ ounces) fresh or frozen broad beans
  (fava beans)
400g (12½ ounces) canned artichokes,
  drained, halved

TOMATO DRESSING
1 medium tomato (150g), seeded, chopped finely
2 tablespoons finely shredded fresh basil leaves
2 tablespoons olive oil
1 tablespoon white wine vinegar

1 Make tomato dressing.
2 Add shelled broad beans to saucepan of
boiling salted water, boil, uncovered, about
2 minutes or until skins wrinkle; drain. Transfer
to bowl of iced water, stand 2 minutes; drain.
3 Peel broad beans. Place beans in medium
bowl with artichokes and dressing; toss gently
to combine. Season to taste.

tomato dressing Combine ingredients in small
bowl; season to taste.

prep + cook time 20 minutes **serves** 4
nutritional count per serving 9.5g total fat
(1.5g saturated fat); 539kJ (129 cal); 4.4g
carbohydrate; 6.1g protein; 10.6g fibre

YOU WILL NEED ABOUT 1.25KG
[2.75 POUNDS] FRESH BROAD
BEANS FOR THIS RECIPE.

MOUSSAKA

¼ cup (60ml) olive oil
2 large eggplants(aubergine) (1kg), sliced thinly
1 large brown onion (200g), chopped finely
2 cloves garlic, crushed
1kg (2 pounds) minced lamb
410g (13 ounces) canned chopped tomatoes
½ cup (125ml) dry white wine
1 teaspoon ground cinnamon
¼ cup (20g) finely grated kefalotyri cheese

WHITE SAUCE

75g (2½ ounces) butter
⅓ cup (50g) plain (all-purpose) flour
2 cups (500ml) milk

1 Heat oil in large frying pan; cook eggplant, in batches, until browned both sides. Drain on absorbent paper.
2 Cook onion and garlic in same pan, stirring, until onion softens. Add lamb; cook, stirring, until lamb changes colour. Stir in undrained tomatoes, wine and cinnamon; bring to the boil. Reduce heat; simmer, uncovered, about 30 minutes or until liquid has evaporated.
3 Meanwhile, preheat oven to 180°C/350°F. Oil shallow 2-litre (8-cup) rectangular baking dish.
4 Make white sauce.
5 Place one-third of the eggplant, overlapping slices slightly, in dish; spread half the meat sauce over eggplant. Repeat layering with another third of the eggplant, remaining meat sauce and remaining eggplant. Spread white sauce over top layer of eggplant; sprinkle with cheese.
6 Bake moussaka about 40 minutes or until top browns lightly. Cover; stand 10 minutes before serving.

white sauce Melt butter in medium saucepan, add flour; cook, stirring, until mixture bubbles and thickens. Gradually add milk; stir until mixture boils and thickens.

prep + cook time 1 hour 50 minutes **serves** 6
nutritional count per serving 36.6g total fat (16.5g saturated fat); 2420kJ (579 cal); 18g carbohydrate; 41.8g protein; 5.3g fibre

serving suggestion Serve with a green salad.

SLOW-COOKED POTATOES WITH WINE AND HERBS

1 medium lemon (140g)

600g (1¼ pounds) new potatoes,
  halved lengthways

1 tablespoon olive oil

1 medium brown onion (150g), sliced thinly

12 unpeeled garlic cloves

1 tablespoon rigani

4 bay leaves

½ cup (125ml) dry white wine

1 cup (250ml) chicken stock

⅓ cup (50g) kalamata olives

⅓ cup (65g) feta cheese, crumbled

1 Preheat oven to 160°C/325°F.

2 Finely grate rind from the lemon. Squeeze lemon; you need ¼ cup juice. Combine potatoes and juice in bowl; season.

3 Heat oil in medium baking dish; cook onion and garlic, stirring, until onion softens. Add potatoes with juice, rigani, rind and bay leaves; stir to coat in onion mixture. Add wine and stock; bring to the boil.

4 Roast potato mixture, uncovered, in oven, stirring occasionally, about 40 minutes or until potatoes are tender.

5 Serve potatoes with olives and cheese.

prep + cook time 55 minutes **serves** 4 (as a side)

nutritional count per serving 11g total fat (3.6g saturated fat); 970kJ (232 cal); 22.8g carbohydrate; 8g protein; 5.3g fibre

GRILLED LEMON CHICKEN

½ cup (125ml) olive oil
½ cup (125ml) lemon juice
1.5kg (3 pounds) chicken thigh fillets
2 teaspoons rigani
2 teaspoons coarse cooking salt (kosher salt)
1 teaspoon ground white pepper
1 medium lemon (140g), cut into wedges

1 Blend or process oil and juice until thick and creamy.
2 Combine chicken, rigani, salt, pepper and half the lemon mixture in medium bowl. Thread chicken onto eight oiled metal skewers.
3 Cook skewers on heated oiled grill plate (or grill or barbecue or grill pan), brushing frequently with remaining lemon mixture until cooked through.
4 Serve skewers with lemon wedges.

prep + cook time 30 minutes **serves** 8
nutritional count per serving 30g total fat (7g saturated fat); 1690kJ (404 cal); 1g carbohydrate; 33g protein; 0.1g fibre

serving suggestion Serve with a green salad

STUFFED EGGPLANT WITH LAMB AND RICE

2 large eggplants (1kg), halved
¼ cup (60ml) olive oil
1 medium brown onion (150g), chopped finely
300g (9½ ounces) minced (ground) lamb
3 cloves garlic, crushed
⅓ cup (65g) medium-grain rice
½ cup (125ml) water
1 tablespoon lemon juice
2 teaspoons rigani (Greek oregano)
⅔ cup (50g) coarsely grated kefalograviera cheese

1 Preheat oven to 220°C/425°F.
2 Cut a 1cm (½-inch) border inside each eggplant; scoop out flesh without breaking skin. Place eggplant shells on oven tray; brush with 1 tablespoon of the oil. Roast about 20 minutes or until tender.
3 Meanwhile, coarsely chop eggplant flesh. Heat 1 tablespoon of the oil in medium frying pan; cook eggplant, stirring, until tender. Remove from pan.
4 Heat remaining oil in same pan; cook onion, stirring, until softened. Add lamb; cook, stirring, until browned. Add garlic, cook, stirring, until fragrant. Return eggplant to pan with rice and the water; cook, covered, over low heat, about 10 minutes or until rice is tender. Stir in juice and rigani; season to taste.
5 Spoon lamb mixture into eggplant shells; sprinkle with cheese. Bake about 20 minutes or until cheese is browned.

prep + cook time 1 hour **serves** 4
nutritional count per serving 28.4g total fat (8.5g saturated fat); 1800kJ (430 cal); 20.5g carbohydrate; 23.6g protein; 7.2g fibre

serving suggestion Serve with a Greek salad.

ROAST LEG OF LAMB WITH POTATOES AND ARTICHOKES

1.2kg (2½-pound) leg of lamb
2 cloves garlic, sliced
6 small unpeeled potatoes (720g), quartered
1 medium lemon (140g), quartered
3 sprigs fresh thyme
1½ tablespoons olive oil
400g (12½ ounces) canned artichokes
   in brine, drained

1 Preheat oven to 240°C/450°F.
2 Pierce lamb all over with small sharp knife; press garlic into cuts.
3 Place lamb in large baking dish. Place potatoes, lemon and thyme in single layer around lamb; season. Rub oil over lamb and potatoes. Roast, uncovered, 20 minutes. Reduce oven to 200°C/400°F; roast, uncovered, about 30 minutes or until lamb is cooked as desired. Remove lamb from dish; stand, covered, 15 minutes.
4 Meanwhile, increase oven to 220°C/425°F. Add artichokes to dish; roast, uncovered, 15 minutes.
5 Serve lamb sliced with potatoes and artichokes.

prep + cook time 1 hour 25 minutes **serves** 4
nutritional count per serving 23g total fat (7g saturated fat); 2145kJ (512 cal); 24.4g carbohydrate; 51.8g protein; 9.7g fibre

note For this cooking time, the lamb will be pink.
If you prefer it well done, roast a further 20 minutes at 200°C/400°F.

RABBIT WITH OLIVES, PARSLEY AND PINE NUTS

1.4kg (2¾-pound) whole rabbit
1 cup (150g) feta-stuffed green olives
½ cup loosely packed fresh flat-leaf parsley leaves
⅓ cup (50g) pine nuts, roasted
1½ cups (375ml) dry white wine
½ cup (125ml) water
½ cup (125ml) olive oil
2 teaspoons finely chopped fresh rosemary

1 Preheat oven to 160°C/325°F. Oil large baking dish.
2 Rinse rabbit under cold water; pat dry inside and out with absorbent paper. Place rabbit in baking dish; fill cavity of rabbit with combined olives, parsley and pine nuts. Tie at intervals with kitchen string.
3 Combine wine, the water, oil and rosemary in small jug; pour over rabbit. Season with salt and black pepper.
4 Roast rabbit about 1½ hours or until rabbit is tender. Serve rabbit drizzled with pan juices.

prep + cook time 1 hour 45 minutes **serves** 4
nutritional count per serving 54.3g total fat (9g saturated fat); 3098kJ (740 cal); 2.4g carbohydrate; 53g protein; 2.1g fibre

serving suggestions Serve with a green salad and crusty bread.

GOAT AND CAPSICUM STEW

¼ cup (60ml) olive oil

1.6kg (3¼-pound) boneless goat shoulder,
  chopped coarsely

2 medium brown onions (300g), sliced thinly

1 bay leaf

400g (12½ ounces) canned chopped tomatoes

½ cup (125ml) chicken stock

2 teaspoons rigani (Greek oregano)

2 medium red capsicums (bell peppers) (400g),
  sliced thinly

1 medium yellow capsicum (bell pepper) (200g),
  sliced thinly

2 tablespoons coarsely chopped flat-leaf parsley

1 Heat 2 tablespoons of the oil in large
saucepan; cook goat, in batches, until browned.
Remove from pan.

2 Heat remaining oil in same pan; cook onion
and bay leaf, stirring, until onion softens. Return
goat to pan with undrained tomatoes, stock and
rigani; bring to the boil. Reduce heat; simmer,
covered, 2½ hours.

3 Stir in capsicum; simmer, covered, 20 minutes
or until capsicum is tender. Season to taste.

4 Serve stew sprinkled with parsley.

prep + cook time 3 hours 15 minutes **serves** 6
nutritional count per serving 17.5g total fat
(4.1g saturated fat); 2105kJ (503 cal); 6.9g
carbohydrate; 74.5g protein; 3.3g fibre

serving suggestions Serve with steamed rice or
mashed potatoes.

GOAT SHOULDER IS GOOD FOR STEWS AND
CASSEROLES AS IT NEEDS LONG SLOW
COOKING TO BE TENDER. IT IS SOLD IN
GREEK AND SPECIALTY BUTCHERS AND
OFTEN COMES FROZEN. ASK THE BUTCHER
TO CUT THE MEAT INTO CHUNKS WHILE
FROZEN; THAW THE MEAT IN THE
REFRIGERATOR AT HOME.

GOAT KLEFTIKO

1.5kg (3-pound) goat shoulder
3 cloves garlic, sliced
2 tablespoons olive oil
¼ cup coarsely chopped fresh oregano
1 tablespoon finely grated lemon rind
2 tablespoons lemon juice
90g (3 ounces) kefalograviera cheese,
  sliced thickly

1 Preheat oven to 170°C/340°F.
2 Pierce goat all over with small sharp knife, press garlic into cuts; season. Heat oil in large frying pan; cook goat until browned.
3 Layer two sheets of baking paper; fold into quarters then open. Place paper in large baking dish; place goat in centre of creases. Sprinkle goat with oregano and rind; drizzle with juice. Top with cheese; fold paper over to enclose, sealing edges to avoid juices escaping. Wrap in foil.
4 Roast goat about 2½ hours or until goat is tender. Stand 15 minutes before serving.

prep + cook time 3 hours (+ standing) **serves** 4
nutritional count per serving 10.5g total fat (3.6g saturated fat); 1045kJ (250 cal); 0.4g carbohydrate; 36.3g protein; 0.3g fibre

notes Goat is sold in Greek and specialty butchers and often comes frozen. The leg of goat will give more meat than the shoulder and will take up to 4 hours to roast. The name kleftiko comes from the "klephts", bandits who used to roam the Greek countryside, stealing goats and lambs and then cooking them in a sealed pit to avoid any smoke being seen. Nowadays, the meat is cooked in a parcel or in a clay pot dish. This method ensures that all the juices and moisture remain and the meat falls off the bone.

serving suggestions Serve with pan-fried potatoes and a green salad.

LEMON AND GARLIC LAMB KEBABS

8 x 15cm (6-inch) stalks fresh rosemary
750g (1½ pounds) lamb fillets,
  cut into 3cm (1¼-inch) pieces
3 cloves garlic, crushed
2 tablespoons olive oil
2 teaspoons finely grated lemon rind
1 tablespoon lemon juice

1 Remove leaves from bottom two-thirds of each rosemary stalk; sharpen trimmed ends to a point.
2 Thread lamb onto rosemary skewers. Brush kebabs with combined garlic, oil, rind and juice. Cover; refrigerate until required.
3 Cook kebabs on heated oiled grill plate (or grill or barbecue), brushing frequently with remaining garlic mixture, until cooked.

prep + cook time 30 minutes **serves** 4
nutritional count per serving 15.9g total fat (4.3g saturated fat); 1250kJ (299 cal); 0.4g carbohydrate; 38.6g protein; 0.4g fibre

serving suggestion Serve with a Greek salad.

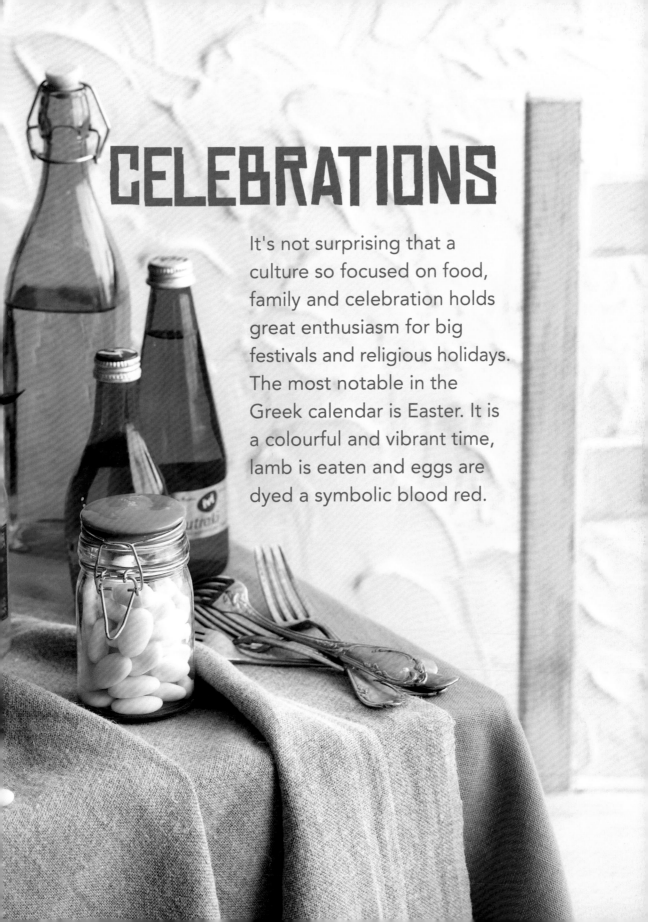

CELEBRATIONS

It's not surprising that a culture so focused on food, family and celebration holds great enthusiasm for big festivals and religious holidays. The most notable in the Greek calendar is Easter. It is a colourful and vibrant time, lamb is eaten and eggs are dyed a symbolic blood red.

EASTER CHEESE PIES [FLAOUNES]

2 teaspoons (7g) dry yeast
1 cup (250ml) warm water
1 cup (250ml) warm milk
1 teaspoon salt
2 teaspoons caster sugar
5 cups (750g) plain (all-purpose) flour
2 tablespoons olive oil
40g (1½ ounces) butter, melted
1 egg, beaten lightly
¼ cup (35g) sesame seeds

CHEESE FILLING

2 cups (250g) coarsely grated kasseri cheese
1⅓ cups (180g) coarsely grated haloumi cheese
1 tablespoon semolina
2 tablespoons finely chopped fresh mint
4 eggs

1 Combine yeast, the water, milk, salt and sugar in small bowl. Cover; stand in warm place about 10 minutes or until frothy.
2 Sift flour into large bowl, stir in yeast mixture, then oil and butter; mix to soft dough. Knead dough on floured surface about 5 minutes or until smooth and elastic. Place dough in large oiled bowl, turn to coat. Cover; stand in warm place about 1 hour or until doubled in size.
3 Meanwhile, preheat oven to 220°C/425°F. Oil four oven trays; line with baking paper.
4 Make cheese filling.
5 Knead dough on floured surface 2 minutes. Working with half the dough at a time, roll dough to 5mm (¼-inch) thick; cut out 10.5cm (4¼-inch) rounds. Drop level tablespoons of filling into centre of each round; brush edge with egg. Shape into a triangle by folding over three sides; pinch edges together, leaving a little filling exposed.
6 Place pies on trays 3cm (1¼ inches) apart; brush with more egg, sprinkle with seeds.
7 Bake pies about 15 minutes or until browned and puffed. Serve warm or cold.

cheese filling Combine ingredients in medium bowl; season.

prep + cook time 1 hour (+ standing) **makes** 32
nutritional count per pie 6.8g total fat (3.1g saturated fat); 686kJ (164 cal); 18.3g carbohydrate; 7.4g protein; 1g fibre

EASTER BREAD [TSOUREKI]

6 teaspoons (21g) dry yeast
½ cup (125ml) warm water
1 cup (250ml) warm milk
1 teaspoon salt
1 teaspoon caster sugar
155g (5 ounces) butter, softened
2 teaspoons finely grated lemon rind
1 cup (220g) caster sugar, extra
4 eggs
6 cups (900g) plain (all-purpose) flour
2 teaspoons ground cinnamon
1 egg yolk, extra
¼ cup (20g) flaked almonds

1 Combine yeast, the water, half the milk, salt and sugar in small bowl. Cover; stand in warm place about 10 minutes or until frothy.

2 Beat butter, rind and extra sugar in small bowl with electric mixer until light and fluffy. Beat in eggs, one at a time, then remaining cooled milk (mixture will curdle at this stage, but will come together later).

3 Sift flour and cinnamon into large bowl, stir in yeast and butter mixtures; mix to a soft dough. Knead dough on floured surface about 5 minutes or until smooth and elastic. Place dough in large greased bowl. Cover; stand in warm place about 1 hour or until doubled in size.

4 Meanwhile, preheat oven to 220°C/425°F. Grease two oven trays; line with baking paper.

5 Knead dough on floured surface 2 minutes. Divide dough in half, divide each half into thirds. Roll each third into sausage-shaped lengths of about 45cm (18 inches). Plait three lengths together, shape into a ring. Repeat with remaining lengths. Place on trays; cover, stand in warm place about 30 minutes or until doubled in size.

6 Brush bread with extra egg yolk, sprinkle with nuts.

7 Bake 20 minutes, reduce oven to 180°C/350°F; bake further 20 minutes or until browned. Cool on tray 5 minutes. Serve warm or cold.

prep + cook time 1 hour 30 minutes (+ standing)
serves 16
nutritional count per serving 10.9g total fat (5.9g saturated fat); 1496kJ (357 cal); 56.3g carbohydrate; 8.8g protein; 2.5g fibre

notes A few red-dyed, hard-boiled eggs can also be positioned at even intervals when plaiting the dough. You could also decorate the bread with sesame seeds or slivered almonds.

EASTER BUTTER BISCUITS [KOULOURAKIA]

125g (4 ounces) butter, melted
1 teaspoon vanilla extract
2 teaspoons finely grated orange rind
⅔ cup (150g) caster sugar
2 eggs
2 tablespoons milk
3 cups (450g) self-raising flour
1 egg yolk, extra
2 tablespoons sesame seeds
¼ cup (35g) flaked almonds

1 Preheat oven to 180°C/350°F. Grease oven trays; line with baking paper.
2 Beat butter, extract, rind and sugar in small bowl with electric mixer until combined. Beat in eggs, one at a time; do not over-beat. Transfer mixture to large bowl; stir in milk and sifted flour, in two batches. Turn dough onto floured surface; knead lightly until smooth.
3 Divide dough into 10 balls, divide each ball into five balls. Roll each ball into 15cm (6-inch) sausage-shaped lengths, then cut into 10cm (4-inch) lengths. Shape lengths into scrolls, twists and figure eights; place about 2.5cm (1 inch) apart on trays. Brush with extra egg yolk, sprinkle with seeds and nuts.
4 Bake biscuits about 15 minutes; cool on trays.

prep + cook time 1 hour **makes** 50
nutritional count per biscuit 3g total fat (1.5g saturated fat); 300kJ (72 cal); 9.6g carbohydrate; 1.6g protein; 0.5g fibre

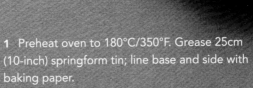

MOIST CARROT AND APPLE CAKE

2 cups (300g) self-raising flour
1 teaspoon bicarbonate of soda (baking soda)
1 cup (220g) caster sugar
4 cups (960g) coarsely grated carrot
2 cups (340g) coarsely grated apple
1 tablespoon finely grated orange rind
¼ cup (60ml) orange juice
¾ cup (180ml) olive oil
⅓ cup (80ml) brandy
1 cup (150g) roasted pine nuts
2 teaspoons icing sugar

1 Preheat oven to 180°C/350°F. Grease 25cm (10-inch) springform tin; line base and side with baking paper.
2 Sift flour and soda into large bowl; stir in caster sugar, carrot, apple and rind. Stir in juice, oil, brandy and pine nuts. Pour mixture into pan.
3 Bake cake about 1 hour. Stand cake 10 minutes before removing from springform tin. Serve dusted with sifted icing sugar.

prep + cook time 1 hour 20 minutes (+ standing)
serves 12
nutritional count per serving 22.8g total fat (2.8g saturated fat); 1720kJ (410 cal); 44.5g carbohydrate; 5g protein; 5.3g fibre

HALVA

2 cups (440g) caster sugar
1 litre (4 cups) water
2 cloves
1 cinnamon stick
220g (7 ounces) butter, chopped coarsely
2 cups (320g) semolina
½ cup (80g) coarsely chopped blanched almonds
2 teaspoons finely grated orange rind
½ cup (80g) coarsely chopped raisins
¼ cup (40g) blanched whole almonds, roasted
1 teaspoon ground cinnamon

1 Grease 20cm x 30cm (8-inch x 12-inch) slice pan or ovenproof dish; line base with baking paper, extending paper 5cm (2 inches) over short sides.
2 Stir sugar, the water, cloves and cinnamon stick in medium saucepan over heat until sugar dissolves. Bring to the boil; boil, uncovered, without stirring, 5 minutes. Cool 5 minutes.
3 Meanwhile, heat butter in large saucepan until foaming. Add semolina and chopped nuts; cook, stirring, about 8 minutes or until lightly browned. Remove from heat. Carefully strain sugar syrup into semolina mixture (mixture will bubble up).
4 Return pan to heat, add rind and raisins; cook, stirring, about 1 minute or until thick and starting to come away from the side of the pan.
5 Spread semolina mixture into pan; top with extra nuts, cool. Sprinkle with ground cinnamon before cutting.

prep + cook time 30 minutes (+ standing)
serves 20
nutritional count per serving 12.4g total fat (6g saturated fat); 1097kJ (262 cal); 36g carbohydrate; 3g protein; 1.3g fibre

SWEETS

BAKLAVA

1½ cups (200g) shelled unsalted pistachio nuts

2 cups (200g) walnut pieces

¼ cup (55g) caster sugar

2 tablespoons fine semolina

1 teaspoon ground cinnamon

pinch ground cloves

375g (12 ounces) filo pastry

310g (10 ounces) butter, melted

30 whole cloves

SYRUP

1 cup (220g) caster sugar

1 cup (250ml) water

¼ cup (90g) honey

1 tablespoon lemon juice

1 cinnamon stick

1 Preheat oven to 200°C/400°F. Grease 20cm x 30cm (8-inch x 12-inch) lamington pan.

2 Process nuts, sugar, semolina, cinnamon and ground cloves until chopped finely; transfer to medium bowl.

3 Brush 1 sheet of pastry with a little of the butter; top with 7 more sheets, brushing each well with butter. Fold pastry in half, place into pan. Sprinkle pastry with thin even layer of the nut mixture. Layer another 2 sheets of pastry, brushing each well with more butter. Fold pastry in half, place in pan; top with another layer of nut mixture. Repeat layering process until all nut mixture has been used. Repeat layering and buttering with any remaining pastry sheets; brush the final layer with butter. Score the top lightly in diamond pattern; press one whole clove into centre of each piece.

4 Bake baklava about 50 minutes.

5 Meanwhile, make syrup.

6 Pour syrup over hot baklava. Cool before cutting.

syrup Stir ingredients in small saucepan over heat until sugar dissolves; bring to the boil. Reduce heat; simmer, uncovered, about 10 minutes or until thickened slightly. Discard cinnamon; cool syrup.

prep + cook time 1 hour 20 minutes (+ cooling)
makes 30
nutritional count per piece 16.4g total fat (6.1g saturated fat); 1010kJ (240 cal); 21g carbohydrate; 3.6g protein; 1.4g fibre

WHEN WORKING WITH THE FIRST EIGHT
SHEETS OF FILO PASTRY, COVER THE
REMAINING SHEETS WITH A PIECE OF
BAKING PAPER THEN A DAMP TEA TOWEL
TO PREVENT THEM DRYING OUT.

HONEY WALNUT BISCUITS

1 cup (250ml) vegetable oil
½ cup (110g) caster sugar
½ cup (125ml) orange juice
2 tablespoons brandy
1 egg
4 cups (600g) self-raising flour
1 cup (160g) fine semolina
1 teaspoon ground cinnamon
1 cup (100g) walnut pieces, chopped finely

SPICED SYRUP

1 cup (220g) caster sugar
½ cup (175g) honey
½ cup (125ml) water
2 tablespoons lemon juice
1 cinnamon stick
6 cloves

1 Preheat oven to 160°C/325°F. Grease oven trays; line with baking paper.
2 Combine oil, sugar, juice, brandy and egg in large bowl. Stir in sifted flour, semolina and half the cinnamon.
3 Roll level tablespoons of mixture into 6cm (2½-inch) oval shapes. Place on trays, about 4cm (1½ inches) apart.
4 Bake biscuits about 25 minutes. Cool on trays.
5 Meanwhile, make spiced syrup.
6 Dip biscuits, in batches, into hot syrup for about 30 seconds or until well coated; transfer to wire rack. Sprinkle biscuits with combined walnuts and remaining cinnamon. Cool.

spiced syrup Stir ingredients in small saucepan over heat until sugar dissolves; bring to the boil. Reduce heat; simmer, uncovered, about 7 minutes or until thickened slightly. Strain syrup into heatproof bowl.

prep + cook time 55 minutes (+ cooling)
makes 48
nutritional count per biscuit 15.8g total fat (1.8g saturated fat); 1545kJ (370 cal); 51.8g carbohydrate; 5.2g protein; 1.8g fibre

MILOPITA

3 medium apples (450g), peeled, cored, quartered
¼ cup (60ml) lemon juice
60g (2 ounces) butter
¼ cup (55g) firmly packed light brown sugar
1 teaspoon ground cinnamon
125g (4 ounces) butter, softened, extra
1 cup (220g) caster sugar
1 tablespoon finely grated lemon rind
1 teaspoon vanilla extract
2 eggs, separated
1 cup (150g) self-raising flour
¼ cup (60ml) milk
1 tablespoon icing sugar

BRANDY YOGURT

1½ tablespoons brandy
3 teaspoons light brown sugar
1 cup (280g) Greek-style yogurt

1 Preheat oven to 160°C/325°F. Grease 24cm (9½-inch) fluted pie dish.
2 Slice apple thinly; combine in medium bowl with juice. Stir butter, brown sugar and cinnamon in small saucepan over heat until sugar dissolves.
3 Beat extra butter, caster sugar, rind, extract and egg yolks in small bowl with electric mixer until light and fluffy. Stir in sifted flour and milk, in two batches.
4 Beat egg whites in small bowl with electric mixer until soft peaks form; fold into cake mixture, in two batches. Spread mixture into dish.
5 Drain apples; discard juice, return apples to bowl. Stir warm brown sugar mixture into apples. Arrange apple slices over batter in dish; drizzle with brown sugar mixture. Bake about 45 minutes.
6 Meanwhile, make brandy yogurt.
7 Dust milopita with sifted icing sugar; serve warm with brandy yogurt.

brandy yogurt Stir brandy and sugar in small bowl until sugar dissolves; stir in yogurt.

prep + cook time 1 hour 30 minutes **serves** 8
nutritional count per serving 22.5g total fat (14.2g saturated fat); 1962kJ (470 cal); 61.1g carbohydrate; 6.2g protein; 1.8g fibre

GREEK COFFEE

1 cup (250ml) cold water
1½ tablespoons ground greek coffee
3 teaspoons caster sugar

1 Place the water in 4-demitasse-cup capacity
briki or small saucepan. Add coffee and sugar;
stir over low heat until sugar dissolves. Slowly
bring to the boil; remove from heat when froth
almost reaches the top of briki.
2 Divide froth among four demitasse cups,
then carefully fill with remaining coffee mixture.
Serve immediately with a glass of cold water.

prep + cook time 10 minutes **serves** 4
nutritional count per serving 0g total fat (0g
saturated fat); 107kJ (26 cal); 6g carbohydrate;
0.6g protein; 0.7g fibre

notes A traditional briki (small pot) is the best
pot to use when making Greek coffee because
it allows the proper amount of froth to form
which in turn adds to the unique taste. Brikis
are available from Greek and Middle Eastern
delicatessens. A demitasse cup holds about
¼ cup (60ml).

CHEESECAKE WITH BRANDIED MUSCATELS

125g (4 ounces) sponge finger biscuits

50g (1½ ounces) unsalted butter, melted

500g (1 pound) unsalted fresh myzithra cheese

½ cup (80g) icing sugar

1 tablespoon finely grated lemon rind

1 tablespoon cornflour

4 eggs

½ cup (125ml) double cream

2 tablespoons flaked almonds,
   chopped coarsely

BRANDIED MUSCATELS

¾ cup (165g) firmly packed light brown sugar

¼ cup (60ml) water

¼ cup (60ml) brandy

1 tablespoon honey

12 small clusters muscatels

1 Preheat oven to 140°C/280°F. Grease 20cm (8-inch) round springform tin; line base and side with baking paper.

2 Process biscuits until fine. Add butter, process until combined. Press mixture firmly over base of tin. Refrigerate 30 minutes.

3 Meanwhile, beat cheese, sifted icing sugar, rind and cornflour in small bowl with electric mixer until smooth. Beat in eggs, one at a time; beat in cream, in two batches. Pour mixture into tin; sprinkle with nuts.

4 Bake cheesecake about 1 hour 10 minutes. Turn oven off; leave to cool completely in oven with door ajar. Cover; refrigerate 1 hour.

5 Meanwhile, make brandied muscatels.

6 Serve cheesecake topped with muscatels and drizzled with syrup.

brandied muscatels Stir sugar, the water, brandy and honey in small saucepan over heat until sugar dissolves; bring to the boil. Reduce heat; simmer, uncovered, without stirring, about 5 minutes or until thickened slightly. Add muscatels; cool.

prep + cook time 1 hour 40 minutes (+ cooling & refrigeration) **serves** 12
nutritional count per serving 29.4g total fat (17.6g saturated fat); 1775kJ (424 cal); 34.5g carbohydrate; 5.1g protein; 0.5g fibre

MYZITHRA CHEESE IS THE TRADITIONAL GREEK CHEESE USED IN THIS CHEESECAKE; YOU COULD USE MASCARPONE AS A SUBSTITUTE.

GLOSSARY

ALLSPICE also called jamaican pepper or pimento; tastes like a combination of nutmeg, cumin, clove and cinnamon. Sold whole or ground.

ALMONDS
blanched brown skins removed.
flaked paper-thin slices.
slivered small pieces cut lengthways.

BAKING PAPER also known as parchment paper or baking parchment; a silicone-coated paper that is used for lining baking pans and oven trays so cakes and biscuits won't stick, making removal easy.

BAY LEAVES aromatic leaves from the bay tree available fresh or dried; adds a strong, slightly peppery flavour.

BEANS
borlotti also called roman beans or pink beans, can be eaten fresh or dried. Interchangeable with pinto beans due to their similarity in appearance – pale pink or beige with dark red streaks.
broad (fava beans) also called windsor and horse beans; available dried, fresh, canned and frozen. Fresh should be peeled twice (discarding both the outer long green pod and the beige-green tough inner shell); the frozen beans have had their pods removed but the beige shell still needs removal.

BEETROOT (BEETS) also called red beets; firm, round root vegetable. Use disposable gloves when handling beetroot to prevent your hands becoming stained.

BICARBONATE OF SODA (BAKING SODA) a raising agent.

BUTTER we use salted butter unless stated otherwise; 125g is equal to 1 stick (4 ounces).

CAPERS the grey-green buds of a warm climate (usually Mediterranean) shrub, sold either dried and salted or pickled in a vinegar brine. Capers should be rinsed before using.

CAPSICUM (BELL PEPPER) also known as peppers. Discard seeds and membranes before use.

CHEESE
feta Greek in origin; a crumbly textured goat- or sheep-milk cheese having a sharp, salty taste. Ripened and stored in salted whey; particularly good cubed and tossed into salads.
haloumi a firm, traditionally sheep-milk cheese (but there are also goat's or cow's-milk varieties) with a minty, salty flavour; it does not break down when cooked, however, it should be eaten while still warm as it becomes tough and rubbery on cooling. While it is a Cypriot cheese, it is often used in Greek cooking.
kasseri a medium hard, mild flavoured sheep-milk cheese (it sometimes has a little goat's milk). It's stringy, rather than crumbly and is great for sandwiches or baking. Can be replaced with provolone.
kefalograviera a hard, salty, sheep or cow's-milk cheese. Its flavour is milder than kefalotyri. Can be replaced with pecorino.
kefalotyri a hard, salty cheese made from sheep and/or goat's milk. Its colour varies from white to yellow depending on the mixture of milk used in the process and its age. Great for grating over pasta or salads. Can be replaced with parmesan.
mascarpone an Italian fresh cultured-cream product made in much the same way as yogurt. Whiteish to creamy yellow in colour, with a buttery-rich, luscious texture. Soft, creamy and spreadable, it is

used in Italian desserts and as an accompaniment to fresh fruit.
myzithra (fresh) an unsalted, soft Greek whey cheese with a mild flavour, similar to ricotta and farmer's cheese. Other varieties are also available: sour (made with goat's or sheep milk, yeast and salt) which is similar to provolone; and aged (hard and salty), which is similar to pecorino.
pecorino the generic Italian name for cheeses made from sheep's milk. It's a hard, white to pale yellow cheese. If you can't find it, use parmesan.
provolone a mild stretched-curd cheese similar to mozzarella when young, becoming hard, spicy and grainy the longer it's aged. Golden yellow in colour, with a smooth waxy rind, provolone is a good all-purpose cheese used in cooking, for dessert with cheese, and shredded or flaked.

CHICKEN
marylands leg and thigh still connected in a single piece; bones and skin intact.
thigh fillets thigh with skin and centre bone removed.

CHILLI use disposable gloves when seeding and chopping fresh chillies as they can burn your skin. The seeds contain the heat, so use fewer chillies rather than seeding the lot. **ground** the Asian variety is the hottest, made from dried ground thai chillies; can be used instead of fresh chilli in the proportion of ½ teaspoon ground chilli to 1 medium chopped fresh red chilli.

CINNAMON available both in the piece (called sticks or quills) and ground into powder.

CLOVES dried flower buds of a tropical tree; can be used whole or ground. They have a strong scent and taste so should be used sparingly.

CORNFLOUR (CORNSTARCH) available made from wheat (wheaten cornflour gives a lighter texture in cakes), or 100% corn (maize); used as a thickening agent in cooking.

CREAM
pouring also known as pure or fresh cream. It has no additives and contains a minimum fat content of 35%.
double a whipping cream containing a thickener. Minimum fat content 35%.

CUCUMBER, LEBANESE short, slender and thin-skinned. Probably the most popular variety because of its tender, edible skin, tiny, yielding seeds, and sweet, fresh and flavoursome taste.

CUMIN also called zeera or comino; resembling caraway in size, cumin is the dried seed of a plant related to the parsley family. Has a spicy, almost curry-like flavour. Also available ground.

DRIED CURRANTS tiny, almost black raisins so-named after a grape variety that originated in Corinth, Greece.

EGGPLANT also called aubergine. Ranging in size from tiny to very large and in colour from pale green to deep purple. Can also be purchased char-grilled, packed in oil, in jars.

EGGS we use large chicken eggs weighing an average of 60g unless stated otherwise in the recipes in this book. If a recipe calls for raw or barely cooked eggs, exercise caution if there is a salmonella problem in your area, particularly in food eaten by children and pregnant women.

FENNEL also called finocchio or anise; a crunchy green vegetable slightly resembling celery that's eaten raw in salads, fried as an accompaniment, or used as an ingredient in soups and sauces. Also the name given to the dried seeds of the plant, which have a stronger licorice flavour.

FILO PASTRY paper-thin sheets of raw pastry; brush each sheet with oil or melted butter, stack in layers, then cut and fold as directed.

FLOUR
plain (all-purpose) unbleached wheat flour, is the best for baking: the gluten content ensures a strong dough, producing a light result.
self-raising all-purpose plain or wholemeal flour with baking powder and salt added; make yourself with in the proportion of 1 cup flour to 2 teaspoons baking powder.

KUMARA (ORANGE SWEET POTATO) the Polynesian name of an orange-fleshed sweet potato often confused with yam.

MUSHROOMS, BUTTON small, cultivated white mushrooms with a mild flavour. When a recipe calls for an unspecified type of mushroom, use button.

NUTMEG a strong and pungent spice ground from the dried nut of an evergreen tree native to Indonesia. Usually found ground but the flavour is more intense from a whole nut (available from spice shops), so it's best to grate your own. Used most often in baking and milk-based desserts, but also works nicely in savoury dishes. Often included in mixed spice mixtures.

OIL
olive made from ripened olives.

Extra virgin and virgin are the first and second press, respectively, of the olives and are therefore considered the best; the "extra light" or "light" name on other types refers to taste not fat levels.
peanut pressed from ground peanuts; the most commonly used oil in Asian cooking because of its high smoke point (capacity to handle high heat without burning).
vegetable oils sourced from plant rather than animal fats.

ONION
green (scallion) also called, incorrectly, shallot; an immature onion picked before the bulb has formed, with a long, bright-green edible stalk.
pickling also known as cocktail onions; are baby brown onions, larger than shallots.
red also known as spanish, red spanish or bermuda onion; a sweet-flavoured, large, purple-red onion.
shallots also called french shallots, golden shallots or eschalots. Small and elongated, with a brown skin, they grow in tight clusters similar to garlic.

OREGANO a herb, also known as wild marjoram; has a woody stalk and clumps of tiny, dark-green leaves. Has a pungent, peppery flavour. see also rigano

PINE NUTS also known as pignoli; not a nut but a small, cream-coloured kernel from pine cones. Best roasted before use to bring out the flavour.

PISTACHIOS green, delicately flavoured nuts inside hard off-white shells. Available salted or unsalted in their shells; you can also get them shelled.

POLENTA also known as cornmeal;

a flour-like cereal made of dried corn (maize). Also the dish made from it.

POTATOES
desiree round, smooth white skin and flesh; good for baking and mashing.

russet burbank long and oval, rough white skin with shallow eyes, white flesh; good for baking and frying.

maris piper white skin, oval; good fried, mashed and baked.

RAISINS
dried sweet grapes (traditionally muscatel grapes).

RICE, ARBORIO
small, round-grain rice well-suited to absorb a large amount of liquid; the high level of starch makes it especially suitable
for risottos, giving the dish its classic creaminess.

RIGANO
dried Greek oregano, often sold in bunches; Store dried herbs away from heat or light in airtight packets or containers; do not store in the fridge as transferring from a cold fridge to a warm kitchen then back to the cold, can cause condensation inside the packet and spoil its contents.

ROCKET (ARUGULA)
also called rugula and rucola; peppery green leaf eaten raw in salads or used in cooking. Baby rocket is smaller and less peppery.

SEAFOOD
octopus usually tenderised before you buy them; octopus and squid require either long slow cooking (for large molluscs) or quick cooking over high heat (for small molluscs) – anything in between will make it tough and rubbery.

prawns (shrimp) varieties include, school, king, royal red, Sydney harbour, tiger. Can be bought uncooked (green) or cooked, with or without shells.

sardines also called pilchards; small (up to 18cm long) fish with soft, oily flesh and a strong but pleasant flavour. High in omega-3 fats.

squid also known as calamari; a type of mollusc. Buy squid hoods to make preparation and cooking faster.

SEMOLINA
coarsely ground flour milled from durum wheat; the flour used in making gnocchi, pasta and couscous.

SESAME SEEDS
black and white are the most common of this small oval seed, however there are also red and brown varieties. The seeds are used as an ingredient and as a condiment. Roast the seeds in a heavy-based frying pan over low heat.

SILVER BEET (SWISS CHARD)
also known, incorrectly, as spinach; has fleshy stalks and large leaves, both of which can be prepared as for spinach.

SPINACH
also known as english spinach and, incorrectly, silver beet. Baby spinach leaves are best eaten raw in salads; the larger leaves should be added last to soups, stews and stir-fries, and should be cooked until barely wilted.

SPONGE FINGER BISCUITS
also called savoiardi, savoy biscuits or lady's fingers; Italian-style crisp fingers made from sponge cake mixture.

SUGAR
caster (superfine) finely granulated table sugar.

icing (confectioners') also known as powdered sugar; pulverised granulated sugar crushed together with a small amount of cornflour (cornstarch).

light brown a very soft, finely granulated sugar retaining molasses for its characteristic colour and flavour.

TARAMA
is salt-cured carp or cod roe, available in fish shops.

TOMATOES
canned whole peeled tomatoes in natural juices; available crushed, chopped or diced. Use undrained.

cherry also known as tiny tim or tom thumb tomatoes; small and round tomatoes sometimes sold still on the vine.

paste triple-concentrated tomato puree.

vine (truss) small vine-ripened tomatoes with vine still attached.

VANILLA
beans dried, long, thin pod from a tropical golden orchid; the minuscule black seeds inside the bean are used to impart a luscious vanilla flavour in baking and desserts.

extract obtained from vanilla beans infused in water; a non-alcoholic version of essence.

VINE LEAVES
preserved grapevine leaves are packed in brine, available in cryovac packets from some delicatessens and Middle Eastern food shops; they must be rinsed well and dried before using. Soften fresh leaves in boiling water until pliable then dry before use.

YEAST
(dried and fresh), a raising agent used in dough making. Granular (7g sachets) and fresh compressed (20g blocks) yeast can almost always be substituted one for the other when yeast is called for.

YOGURT
we use plain full-cream yogurt unless stated otherwise.

Greek-style plain yogurt that has been strained in a cloth (traditionally muslin) to remove the whey and to give it a creamy consistency. It is ideal for use in dips and dressings.

ZUCCHINI
also known as courgette; small, pale- or dark-green, yellow or white vegetable belonging to the squash family. Harvested when young, its edible flowers can be used in salads or stuffed and deep-fried.

CONVERSION CHART

MEASURES

One Australian metric measuring cup holds approximately 250ml; one Australian metric tablespoon holds 20ml; one Australian metric teaspoon holds 5ml.

The difference between one country's measuring cups and another's is within a two- or three-teaspoon variance, and will not affect your cooking results. North America, New Zealand and the United Kingdom use a 15ml tablespoon.

All cup and spoon measurements are level. The most accurate way of measuring dry ingredients is to weigh them. When measuring liquids, use a clear glass or plastic jug with the metric markings.

We use large eggs with an average weight of 60g.

DRY MEASURES

METRIC	IMPERIAL
15g	½oz
30g	1oz
60g	2oz
90g	3oz
125g	4oz (¼lb)
155g	5oz
185g	6oz
220g	7oz
250g	8oz (½lb)
280g	9oz
315g	10oz
345g	11oz
375g	12oz (¾lb)
410g	13oz
440g	14oz
470g	15oz
500g	16oz (1lb)
750g	24oz (1½lb)
1kg	32oz (2lb)

LIQUID MEASURES

METRIC	IMPERIAL
30ml	1 fluid oz
60ml	2 fluid oz
100ml	3 fluid oz
125ml	4 fluid oz
150ml	5 fluid oz
190ml	6 fluid oz
250ml	8 fluid oz
300ml	10 fluid oz
500ml	16 fluid oz
600ml	20 fluid oz
1000ml (1 litre)	1¾ pints

LENGTH MEASURES

METRIC	IMPERIAL
3mm	⅛in
6mm	¼in
1cm	½in
2cm	¾in
2.5cm	1in
5cm	2in
6cm	2½in
8cm	3in
10cm	4in
13cm	5in
15cm	6in
18cm	7in
20cm	8in
22cm	9in
25cm	10in
28cm	11in
30cm	12in (1ft)

OVEN TEMPERATURES

The oven temperatures in this book are for conventional ovens; if you have a fan-forced oven, decrease the temperature by 10-20 degrees.

	°C (CELSIUS)	°F (FAHRENHEIT)
Very slow	120	250
Slow	150	300
Moderately slow	160	325
Moderate	180	350
Moderately hot	200	400
Hot	220	425
Very hot	240	475

The imperial measurements used in these recipes are approximate only. Measurements for cake pans are approximate only. Using same-shaped cake pans of a similar size should not affect the outcome of your baking. We measure the inside top of the cake pan to determine sizes.

INDEX

This book is published in 2015 by Bounty Books, a division of Octopus Publishing Group Ltd, based on materials licensed to it by Bauer Media Books, Australia

First published in 2012 by Bauer Media Books

Bauer Media Books is a division of Bauer Media Pty Limited.

54 Park St, Sydney; GPO Box 4088, Sydney, NSW 2001, Australia

phone (+61) 2 9282 8618; fax (+61) 2 9126 3702

www.awwcookbooks.com.au

BAUER MEDIA BOOKS
General manager Christine Whiston
Editor-in-chief Susan Tomnay
Creative director Hieu Chi Nguyen
Art director & designer Hannah Blackmore
Senior editor Stephanie Kistner
Food director Pamela Clark
Sales & rights director Brian Cearnes
Acting marketing manager Sonia Scali
Senior business analyst Rebecca Varela
Operations manager David Scotto
Production manager Victoria Jefferys

Cover & additional food photography Dean Wilmot
Cover & additional styling Olivia Blackmore
Photochef Olivia Andrews
Location photography Yianni Aspradakis

The publisher would like to thank George Kambesis and Vula Koutsoukos for providing props.

Published and Distributed in the United Kingdom by Octopus Publishing Group Ltd

An Hachette UK Company
www.hachette.co.uk

Carmelite House, 50 Victoria Embankment, London, EC4Y 0DZ
www.octopusbooks.co.uk

International foreign language rights, Brian Cearnes, Bauer Media Books
bcearnes@bauer-media.com.au

A CIP catalogue record for this book is available from the British Library

ISBN: 978-0-7537-2986 -1

© Bauer Media Pty Ltd 2012

ABN 18 053 273 546

Printed and bound in China

10 9 8 7 6 5 4 3 2 1